From Rags to Riches

A Practical Family Guide to Wealth and Freedom

RICHARD TRILLION MANTEY

Dedication

To my parents —

Thank you for your love, sacrifices, and the foundation you laid. Your example taught me the value of hard work, faith, and resilience. This book is part of your legacy.

And to every family who's ever struggled in silence…

This book is for you.

For the parents, doing their best with what they have.

For the kids growing up believing "just enough" is all there is.

For the ones who dream of more, even when the world tells them to settle.

May this guide help you break the cycle, build something better,

and create a legacy that starts with you and lasts for generations.

Acknowledgment

This book would not exist without the grace of God, whose guidance and provision continue to shape my purpose and direction. To Him be all the glory.

To my parents, thank you for your sacrifices, your strength, and your unwavering faith. Your resilience laid the groundwork for everything I am and hope to pass on. This journey started with you.

To my family and loved ones: your encouragement, patience, and belief in me kept me grounded through every chapter of this process.

To my readers, thank you for opening this book and trusting me with your time. My hope is that these words meet you exactly where you are, and help move you closer to the freedom you deserve.

To my editor, thank you for helping shape these pages with clarity, precision, and care. Your insight made this book stronger and more impactful.

And to every family, every dreamer, and every determined soul reading this now: may your journey be guided by purpose, not pressure. And may you rise, one wise step at a time.

About the Author

Richard Trillion Mantey is a financial wellness advocate, educator, and family-focused wealth mentor committed to helping everyday people break the cycle of stress and scarcity. Growing up without access to financial guidance, he learned firsthand how hard it can be to build stability from the ground up.

Through years of study, hard-earned experience, and transformation, Richard developed a practical approach to wealth—one rooted in clarity, consistency, and community. Today, he helps families worldwide take control of their finances, build lasting habits, and create futures filled with opportunity and peace of mind.

Richard believes wealth isn't just about money—it's about freedom, choices, and the legacy we leave behind.

When he's not writing, coaching, or sharing ideas, you'll find him learning, walking in gratitude, and helping others discover what's truly possible with the right plan and the right mindset.

Preface

Every family has its own story about money.

For some, it's whispered in quiet anxieties at the kitchen table. For others, it's a legacy of hard-won lessons passed down with pride. And for many, it's a subject best avoided altogether; it's too confusing, too overwhelming, and too distant from daily life.

This book was written to change that conversation.

From Rags to Riches isn't about overnight success or complicated financial jargon. It's not about chasing trends or getting rich quick. It's about the simple, practical steps that real families, busy, imperfect, ordinary families, can take to build a foundation of security, confidence, and freedom. It's about understanding that wealth is more than numbers; habits, values, choices, and conversations around the dinner table echoing for generations.

Inside these pages, you won't find grand theories. You'll find stories. Real ones. Stories of people who started small, stayed consistent, and quietly built something remarkable over time. You'll find tools to help you better understand your money, guide your children, and reshape your family's thoughts about the future.

Because no matter where you begin, wealth isn't a privilege; it's a process. And every family deserves to write its own chapter.

Contents

Chapter 1: Understanding Wealth

The True Meaning of Wealth

Wealth is often perceived as the accumulation of money and material possessions, yet its true meaning extends far beyond these superficial measures. True wealth encompasses the richness of experiences, relationships, and the ability to impact the lives of others positively. Many successful individuals, from entrepreneurs to philanthropists, have shared stories of how they discovered that their greatest treasures were not their bank accounts but the connections and legacies they built throughout their lives.

Research in psychology shows that the happiest individuals often define wealth in terms of relationships and community rather than financial gain. A study by the Harvard Study of Adult Development revealed that strong relationships are key predictors of happiness and longevity. These findings highlight that nurturing bonds with family and friends can lead to a fulfilling life, one that is richer than any monetary figure could represent. By focusing on emotional and social wealth, we can redefine our understanding of what it means to be truly prosperous.

To cultivate this deeper sense of wealth, one must take actionable steps. Start by identifying the relationships that matter most to you and invest time in them. Create traditions, engage in meaningful conversations, and share experiences that will strengthen these connections. Additionally, consider how you can give back to your community, as acts of service not only enrich the lives of others but also enhance your own sense of purpose and fulfilment.

Generational wealth is not solely about passing down financial assets; it is also about imparting wisdom, values, and a mindset that prioritises emotional and social intelligence. Families who engage in open discussions about money and its role in their lives tend to produce financially savvy children who understand the importance of holistic wealth. This approach ensures that future generations inherit not just money, but also the tools necessary to build their own wealth in a meaningful way.

In conclusion, redefining wealth requires a shift in perspective from mere financial success to a broader understanding that incorporates relationships, experiences, and community impact. By embracing this holistic view of wealth, we can create a legacy that lasts for generations, one that reflects the true essence of what it means to be rich in life. As we journey from rags to riches, let us remember that the wealth we create is only as valuable as the lives we touch along the way.

The Psychology of Money

Understanding the psychology of money is crucial for anyone looking to achieve financial freedom. Money is not just a tool for transactions; it carries emotional weight and shapes our behaviours. Many people grow up with financial beliefs that are ingrained from childhood, often passed down through generations. This can lead to cycles of poverty or wealth that are hard to break. By recognising these beliefs, we can begin to change our relationship with money and open ourselves to new possibilities.

Consider the story of a woman named Sarah, who inherited her family's financial fears. Growing up, she witnessed her parents struggle with debt and express anxiety about money. As an adult, she found herself repeating these patterns, living paycheck to paycheck, despite her steady income. It wasn't until she sought professional guidance and began to confront her fears that she realised the power of her mindset. By embracing a positive approach to finances, she started saving and investing, ultimately breaking free from the cycle.

Scientific studies have shown that our beliefs about money can significantly impact our financial decisions. Cognitive behavioural therapy, for instance, has been effective in helping individuals reassess their views on wealth. When we understand the neural pathways that dictate our financial choices, we can actively work to rewire them. This involves setting specific goals, visualising success, and practising gratitude for what we have, which can lead to healthier financial habits and improved wealth accumulation.

To implement these changes, one can take practical steps that align with a positive money mindset. Start by journaling your financial beliefs and identifying which ones are harmful. Set realistic financial goals that inspire rather than intimidate. Surround yourself with positive influences, whether through books, podcasts, or communities that uplift your financial aspirations. Taking small, consistent actions can lead to significant long-term changes in your financial situation and mindset.

In conclusion, the psychology of money is a powerful aspect of achieving financial freedom. By understanding our beliefs and emotions surrounding money, we can change our behaviours and build generational wealth. Just like Sarah, anyone can break free from limiting beliefs and create a prosperous future for themselves and their families. Remember, financial success is as much about mindset as it is about strategy, and fostering a positive relationship with money is the first step towards lasting wealth.

Common Myths About Wealth

Many people believe that wealth is solely the result of luck or inheritance, but this is a common myth that often discourages hard work and perseverance. Stories abound of individuals who started with nothing and built impressive fortunes through sheer dedication and resourcefulness. For instance, take the story of Howard Schultz, the former CEO of Starbucks, who grew up in a poor family in Brooklyn. His journey illustrates that wealth can be created through determination and innovative thinking, rather than mere chance.

Another prevalent myth is that money is inherently evil or that wealthy individuals are greedy. This misconception can create a divide between different socioeconomic classes. In reality, many wealthy individuals use their resources to effect positive change in their communities. For example, philanthropic efforts by billionaires such as Bill Gates and Warren Buffet demonstrate that wealth can be a powerful tool for good, promoting education and healthcare worldwide.

Furthermore, the idea that financial success is unattainable for the average person is a myth that can perpetuate cycles of poverty. Research has shown that financial literacy and planning can significantly impact one's ability to accumulate wealth. Simple steps, such as budgeting, saving, and investing, can empower anyone to take control of their financial future. Sharing stories of everyday people who have transformed their financial situations through education can inspire others to follow suit.

Additionally, many believe that you need to have a high-paying job to become wealthy. While income is a factor, it is not the only one. The way we manage and grow our money is crucial. For instance, individuals who invest wisely, regardless of their income level, can build significant wealth over time. The story of a teacher who diligently saved and invested can serve as a powerful reminder that consistent financial habits can lead to substantial wealth, irrespective of one's starting point.

Lastly, the myth that one must sacrifice personal happiness to achieve financial success is misleading. Many successful individuals find ways to balance their work and personal lives, leading fulfilling lives while also achieving their financial goals. By embracing a holistic approach to wealth that includes personal well-being and relationships, families can create generational wealth that nurtures both financial and emotional stability, ensuring that future generations thrive.

Chapter 2: The Foundations of Financial Freedom

Establishing a Wealth Mindset

Establishing a wealth mindset is not merely about accumulating riches; it is a profound shift in how we perceive money and its role in our lives. Many people grow up with limiting beliefs about wealth, often viewing it as something unattainable or reserved for the fortunate few. However, by examining our beliefs and reprogramming our thoughts, we can cultivate a mindset that not only welcomes wealth but also attracts it. This transformation begins with understanding the stories we tell ourselves about money, which can either hinder or propel us towards financial freedom.

One powerful story comes from a family who struggled for generations with financial instability. They lived in a cycle of scarcity, believing that wealth was beyond their reach. However, one member decided to change the narrative. By embracing the idea that wealth is a mindset, they began to educate themselves about finances, investing, and creating opportunities. This single decision sparked a transformation that not only changed their life but also laid the foundation for future generations. They learned that adopting a wealth mindset involved recognising their self-worth and understanding that they deserved financial success.

Research supports the idea that our beliefs about money fundamentally shape our financial outcomes. Studies show that individuals with a positive wealth mindset are more likely to take calculated risks, seek new opportunities, and persist in the face of challenges. They understand that setbacks are not failures but rather stepping stones toward success. By cultivating resilience and a proactive approach to financial education, anyone can shift their perspective and create a path towards financial independence.

To establish a wealth mindset, one must take actionable steps. Start by setting clear financial goals that align with your values and aspirations. This practice not only clarifies your vision but also reinforces your commitment to achieving it. Next, surround yourself with mentors and communities that inspire and support your financial journey. Engaging with like-minded individuals can provide encouragement and insight, reinforcing the belief that wealth is attainable. Finally, practice gratitude for what you have while remaining open to the possibilities of what you can achieve.

In conclusion, establishing a wealth mindset is a journey that requires dedication and introspection. By changing the stories we tell ourselves and embracing a proactive approach to financial education, we empower ourselves and our families to build generational wealth. As we shift our mindset towards abundance, we not only enhance our financial prospects but also inspire those around us to do the same. This collective shift can create a ripple effect, transforming not just individual lives but entire communities, fostering a legacy of financial freedom for generations to come.

The Importance of Financial Literacy

Financial literacy is not just a buzzword; it is a crucial life skill that empowers individuals and families to take control of their financial futures. Imagine a single mother, working tirelessly to support her children, suddenly finding herself in a position to invest in a small business. With a basic understanding of financial principles, she can navigate the complexities of budgeting and investing, ultimately transforming her family's financial landscape. This is the power of financial literacy—it opens doors that would otherwise remain closed.

Research shows that individuals with a strong grasp of financial concepts are more likely to save for retirement, invest wisely, and avoid crippling debt. A study conducted by the National Endowment for Financial Education found that those who received financial education were significantly more likely to save for emergencies and make informed investment decisions. This knowledge not only benefits the individual but also has a ripple effect on their families and communities, fostering a culture of financial responsibility and planning for the future.

The journey to financial literacy begins with understanding the basics: budgeting, saving, investing, and debt management. Take the story of a young couple who, after attending a financial literacy workshop, learned to create a budget that allowed them to save for a home. By setting clear financial goals and developing a plan, they were able to move from renting to owning their first home within five years. This step-by-step approach showcases that financial literacy is accessible to everyone, regardless of their current situation.

Furthermore, financial literacy plays a vital role in building generational wealth. Parents who understand the importance of teaching their children about money can instill valuable lessons that last a lifetime. Consider a family that regularly discusses financial goals and savings habits at the dinner table. This open dialogue not only strengthens their bond but also equips the next generation with the tools needed to make sound financial choices, breaking the cycle of poverty and paving the way for future prosperity.

In conclusion, the importance of financial literacy cannot be overstated. It is a foundational skill that equips individuals with the knowledge to make informed financial decisions, fostering a brighter future for themselves and their families. By embracing this knowledge and sharing it with the younger generation, we can create a world where financial freedom is not just a dream, but a reality for all. Financial literacy is not merely a personal benefit; it is a collective movement towards building a financially savvy society that nurtures wealth and opportunity for all.

Setting Clear Financial Goals

Setting clear financial goals is the foundation upon which a secure financial future is built. Imagine a family, once struggling to make ends meet, who sat down together to discuss their dreams. They envisioned a comfortable home, a good education for their children, and the ability to travel. By defining these goals, they transformed vague desires into concrete targets. This practice not only provided them with direction but also instilled a sense of purpose in their financial decisions.

Research shows that people who set specific financial goals are more likely to achieve them. A study conducted by the

Dominican University found that individuals who wrote down their goals were 42% more likely to achieve them than those who simply thought about their aspirations. This statistic highlights the power of clarity and commitment in the goal-setting process. By documenting their objectives, families can track their progress and stay motivated, even when faced with challenges.

To set effective financial goals, families should consider the SMART criteria: Specific, Measurable, Achievable, Relevant, and Time-bound. For example, instead of saying, "We want to save money," a family could specify, "We aim to save £10,000 for a family holiday in two years." This specificity makes it easier to create a plan and stick to it. Emotional connections to these goals, such as the joy of creating lasting memories on a holiday, can further enhance motivation.

Moreover, breaking down larger goals into smaller, manageable steps can prevent feelings of overwhelm. A family might set a monthly savings target, allocate a portion of their income to investments, or plan to reduce unnecessary expenses. Each small victory along the way reinforces the family's commitment and builds confidence. Celebrating these milestones together fosters a sense of unity and shared purpose in the family's financial journey.

In conclusion, setting clear financial goals is not just about the numbers; it's about creating a vision for the future. By involving every family member in the goal-setting process, they not only learn valuable financial skills but also develop a sense of ownership over their financial destiny. As families work towards their goals, they create pathways to generational wealth, ensuring a brighter future for their children and grandchildren. With determination and clarity, any family can turn their dreams into reality.

Chapter 3: Creating a Budget That Works

Understanding Income and Expenses

Understanding income and expenses is fundamental to achieving financial freedom. Many families, regardless of their background, often find themselves living paycheck to paycheck. This scenario is not just about having limited resources; it reflects a lack of awareness regarding the flow of money in and out of their lives. Realising the importance of tracking both income and expenses can empower families to take control of their financial destinies, much like how a farmer monitors the weather to ensure a fruitful harvest.

Consider the story of the Martins, a family that struggled with their finances for years. They often overspent on non-essential items, blissfully unaware of how their spending habits drained their savings. One day, they decided to sit down and create a budget. This simple step illuminated their financial landscape, revealing areas where they could cut back and save. Through disciplined tracking of their income and expenses, they transformed their financial situation, eventually building a solid foundation for future generations.

Science backs the notion that financial literacy is critical for success. Studies have shown that individuals who actively manage their finances tend to experience lower stress levels and improved overall well-being. By understanding the dynamics of income and expenses, families can make informed decisions that lead to long-term financial stability. This understanding is akin to the scientific method: observe, hypothesise, test, and conclude. As families engage in this process, they begin to see their financial lives transform.

Moreover, practical steps can be taken to grasp these concepts better. Start by listing all sources of income, from salaries to side hustles, ensuring that every penny is accounted for. Next, track all expenses, categorising them into essentials and non-essentials. This exercise will provide a clearer picture of spending habits, allowing families to adjust their budgets accordingly. As they become more adept at managing their finances, they will discover opportunities for saving and investing, thus paving the way for generational wealth.

Ultimately, understanding income and expenses is not just about numbers; it is about creating a legacy. Families who engage in this process together foster open communication about financial matters, strengthening their bonds. By cultivating a culture of financial awareness, they set their children up for success, ensuring that the lessons learned are passed down through generations. This journey from rags to riches is not merely about accumulating wealth but about instilling values that lead to lasting prosperity.

The 50/30/20 Rule Explained

The 50/30/20 rule serves as a straightforward yet effective budgeting framework that can empower families to achieve financial stability and growth. It suggests that individuals allocate 50% of their income to necessities, 30% to discretionary spending, and 20% to savings or debt repayment. This simple guideline resonates with many, as it offers a clear structure for managing finances without feeling overwhelmed. By following this rule, families can gain control over their spending, fostering a sense of security and enabling them to plan for a brighter financial future.

Consider the story of the Johnson family, who, after years of struggling with their finances, adopted the 50/30/20 rule. Initially sceptical, they soon discovered how easy it was to track their expenses. By categorising their spending, they identified unnecessary subscriptions and frivolous purchases. This newfound awareness allowed them to reallocate funds towards their children's education and a family vacation, showing that practical steps can lead to significant improvements in quality of life.

Scientific studies back the effectiveness of this budgeting strategy, revealing that structured financial plans can reduce stress and increase overall satisfaction. Research has shown that families who adhere to a budgeting plan feel more in control of their financial situations. This leads to better decision-making and a greater ability to save for future aspirations, whether that be a home, education, or retirement. The 50/30/20 rule is not just a formula; it's a pathway to enhanced emotional well-being and security.

Implementing the 50/30/20 rule requires a few simple steps. Start by calculating your total monthly income and categorising your expenses into needs, wants, and savings. Make adjustments as necessary to ensure that each category aligns with the rule. This may involve cutting back on certain discretionary expenses or finding ways to increase your income. Over time, this disciplined approach to budgeting can lead to substantial savings, enabling families to invest in their future, thus creating generational wealth.

Ultimately, the 50/30/20 rule is more than just a budgeting tool; it's a mindset shift towards financial empowerment. By teaching families how to manage their money effectively, they can break the cycle of financial struggle and build a legacy of wealth for future generations. The emotional satisfaction that comes from knowing you are in control of your finances is invaluable, making this rule a vital component of any family's wealth-building journey.

Tools and Resources for Budgeting

Budgeting is not merely about balancing numbers; it's about creating a roadmap to financial freedom. Many families struggle with money management, often feeling overwhelmed by the complexities of their finances. However, tools and resources for budgeting can simplify this process, making it accessible for everyone. By employing these resources, families can take control of their financial destinies and start building generational wealth.

One of the most effective tools for budgeting is the use of budgeting apps. These digital resources can help track daily expenses, categorize spending, and even set financial goals. For instance, a family might find that by using a budgeting app, they can identify unnecessary spending, such as dining out too frequently. This newfound awareness can lead to more informed financial choices, enabling them to save for a family vacation or a child's education. Stories of families transforming their financial habits through apps are becoming increasingly common, showcasing the power of technology in personal finance.

In addition to apps, traditional methods such as the envelope system remain popular and effective. This method involves allocating cash for specific spending categories into separate envelopes, which limits overspending. A single mother, for example, could allocate funds for groceries, entertainment, and savings into designated envelopes, making it easier to stick to her budget. This tangible approach can be particularly beneficial for those who prefer a hands-on method over digital solutions, providing a sense of control and discipline in spending habits.

Furthermore, educational resources like online courses and workshops can enhance budgeting skills. Many organisations offer free or low-cost financial education programs that empower families to manage their finances better. By participating in these workshops, individuals can learn about topics such as debt management, investment basics, and savings techniques. Real-life success stories of participants who have improved their financial literacy serve as inspiring reminders of the impact that knowledge can have on wealth-building.

Finally, community support plays a crucial role in successful budgeting. Families can engage with local financial groups or online forums to share experiences and tips. The emotional support from a community can foster accountability and motivation, encouraging families to stick to their budgets. Countless individuals have reclaimed their financial lives through shared experiences and communal encouragement, proving that while the journey to financial freedom can be daunting, it is achievable with the right tools and support.

Chapter 4: Saving for the Future

The Power of Compound Interest

Compound interest is often described as the eighth wonder of the world, and for good reason. It allows your money to grow exponentially over time. Imagine a young couple who start saving just a small amount every month. Over the years, thanks to compound interest, their modest investments grow into a substantial nest egg, enabling them to afford their dream home or secure a comfortable retirement. This phenomenon illustrates that small, consistent actions can lead to significant financial outcomes, no matter one's starting point in life.

The science behind compound interest is simple yet powerful. When you invest money, not only does your initial amount earn interest, but the interest itself begins to earn interest over time. This snowball effect can turn even the smallest savings into a sizeable fortune. For instance, a child who starts saving £100 at the age of ten, and continues to save £50 each month until they turn eighteen, can accumulate a substantial amount by the time they reach adulthood. This early start highlights the importance of teaching children the value of saving and investing, ensuring that they are equipped for a financially secure future.

To harness the power of compound interest, one must start early and remain consistent. Setting aside even a small amount regularly can yield impressive results over time. It's about creating a habit of saving, which is as crucial as the amount saved. Many families fail to capitalise on this simple principle, often postponing saving for later in life. By making compound interest work for you, you can lay the foundation for generational wealth that will benefit your descendants long after you're gone.

Stories abound of individuals who transformed their financial futures through the power of compound interest. Consider the tale of a single mother who diligently saved a portion of her paycheck each month. Over the years, her modest savings grew, and she was able to secure her children's education and a comfortable retirement. This narrative serves as a beacon of hope, reminding us that with dedication and foresight, anyone can achieve financial stability and wealth through the magic of compound interest.

In conclusion, the power of compound interest is a fundamental principle that can change lives. It teaches us the importance of starting early, being consistent, and understanding the value of patience in wealth accumulation. As we aspire to build a financially secure future for ourselves and our families, let us embrace this powerful tool. By doing so, we not only improve our own lives but also pave the way for future generations to thrive financially, creating a legacy of wealth and security that lasts for years to come.

Building an Emergency Fund

Building an emergency fund is a crucial step towards financial stability and peace of mind. Imagine a family living from paycheck to paycheck, suddenly faced with an unexpected medical expense or a job loss. The panic that sets in can be overwhelming, but having an emergency fund can act as a safety net, providing the necessary support during tough times. This fund allows families to navigate through financial storms without resorting to high-interest loans or credit cards, which can lead to a cycle of debt that is hard to escape.

The science behind emergency funds is compelling. Studies show that individuals with savings are more resilient in the face of financial shocks. According to research by the Federal Reserve, nearly 40% of Americans would struggle to cover a $400 emergency expense. This statistic highlights the importance of building a fund that can cover at least three to six months' worth of living expenses. By starting small and gradually increasing contributions, anyone can build a robust emergency fund that provides security and reduces anxiety.

Steps to create an emergency fund are straightforward and manageable. Begin by setting a realistic savings goal based on your monthly expenses. Next, open a separate savings account dedicated solely to your emergency fund. Automate transfers to this account every month, treating it like a regular bill. This way, saving becomes a consistent habit rather than an afterthought. Even if you can only spare a small amount each month, every little bit adds up over time, contributing to your overall financial health.

Stories of families who have successfully built their emergency funds can serve as inspiration. Take the case of a single mother who, after facing eviction due to unexpected medical bills, decided to take control of her finances. By budgeting strictly and setting aside a small amount each week, she managed to save enough to cover her rent for several months. This not only provided her with a buffer against future emergencies but also empowered her to make better financial decisions moving forward. Her story illustrates that anyone can achieve financial security with determination and a plan.

In conclusion, building an emergency fund is not just a financial strategy; it is a means of fostering peace of mind and resilience. By understanding the importance of saving, setting realistic goals, and learning from others' experiences, anyone can create a safety net that protects against life's uncertainties. The journey to financial freedom begins with small, consistent steps, and an emergency fund is an essential component of that journey, paving the way for a brighter financial future.

Strategies for Effective Saving

Saving money can often feel like an uphill battle, but with the right strategies, it can become a rewarding journey. Imagine a family, much like yours, who decided to save a small portion of their income each month. Initially, it seemed insignificant, but over time, those small savings compounded into a substantial amount, enabling them to buy their first home. This story illustrates that effective saving doesn't require massive sacrifices; it's about consistency and commitment to a brighter financial future.

One of the most effective strategies for saving is the 'pay yourself first' method. This involves setting aside a portion of your income as soon as you receive it, before you allocate money for expenses. Research shows that people who automate their savings are more likely to succeed in reaching their financial goals. By treating savings like a mandatory expense, you create a habit that leads to financial security.

Think of it as building a safety net that protects you and your family from unforeseen circumstances.

Another strategy is to set specific savings goals. Having a clear target, whether it's for a vacation, a new car, or retirement, gives your savings a purpose. This can be likened to a marathon runner training for a race; without a finish line in sight, it's easy to lose motivation. Share your goals with your family to foster accountability and support, reinforcing the idea that you are in this together. Celebrating milestones along the way can also provide the encouragement needed to keep going.

Additionally, consider the impact of small lifestyle changes on your savings. A family decided to forgo their weekly dining out experience, redirecting those funds into a savings account instead. Over a year, they realised they could save thousands of pounds just by making minor adjustments to their spending habits. This not only contributed to their savings but also promoted a more mindful approach to their finances. It's important to remember that every little bit counts, and small sacrifices can lead to significant rewards over time.

Finally, involve the younger generation in your saving journey. Teaching children about money management early can instil valuable habits that benefit them for life. Use real-life examples to demonstrate the importance of saving and investing, encouraging them to set their own goals. This not only empowers them but also builds a legacy of financial wisdom that can be passed down through generations. By sharing stories of struggle and success, you can inspire your family to engage in their financial future actively.

Chapter 5: Investing Basics

Understanding Different Investment Types

Investing is a journey that can lead to financial freedom, but understanding the different types of investments is crucial. From stocks and bonds to real estate and mutual funds, each investment type has its own unique characteristics, risks, and rewards. For instance, consider the story of a young couple who started investing in stocks. They researched companies, tracked market trends, and gradually built a diversified portfolio. Their experience highlights that informed decision-making is key to successful investing.

Bonds serve as a safer alternative for those who prefer stability over high returns. They are essentially loans made to governments or corporations, and in return, investors receive interest payments. A poignant example is a retired teacher who invested her savings in bonds. This choice provided her with a steady income stream, allowing her to enjoy her retirement without financial worries. Understanding the mechanisms of bonds can empower individuals to make conservative yet fruitful investment decisions.

Real estate is another powerful investment avenue. It not only offers the potential for appreciation but also provides passive income through rental properties. A family who purchased a modest rental property discovered the joy of earning money while sleeping. They learned that, with careful management, real estate can be a reliable source of generational wealth, passed down to their children, ensuring a brighter financial future for their family.

Mutual funds present a great opportunity for those who wish to invest without deep financial knowledge. They pool money from multiple investors to purchase a diversified portfolio of stocks and bonds. An inspiring story is that of a single mother who started investing small amounts in a mutual fund. Over the years, her investment grew significantly, helping her secure her children's education. This illustrates that even modest investments can yield substantial returns over time, reinforcing the idea that every bit counts.

Finally, understanding risk tolerance is essential in making investment choices. Individuals must assess their comfort levels with market fluctuations and potential losses. A young entrepreneur once shared how he learned to embrace risk by investing in startups. His willingness to face uncertainty led to significant rewards, proving that calculated risks can sometimes yield the greatest returns. By recognising their own risk tolerance, investors can tailor their strategies to align with their financial goals, paving the way for a secure and prosperous future.

Risk vs. Reward: Finding Your Balance

In the journey towards financial freedom, understanding the delicate balance between risk and reward is crucial. Many families chase after quick gains, only to find themselves entangled in debts and losses. Consider the story of a young couple who invested their life savings in a trendy start-up, lured by the promise of rapid returns. Their excitement quickly turned to despair when the company folded, leaving them with nothing but regret. This illustrates that while high rewards may be enticing, the associated risks must be carefully weighed before making financial decisions.

Science suggests that taking calculated risks can lead to greater financial success, but it's essential to have a clear strategy. Research indicates that individuals who assess their risk tolerance and diversify their investments tend to accumulate wealth over time. For instance, a family that chooses to invest in a mix of stocks, bonds, and real estate not only protects their capital but also positions themselves for long-term growth. This balanced approach mitigates potential losses while still allowing for the possibility of significant gains.

Steps to finding this balance involve first identifying your financial goals and understanding your comfort level with risk. Families should engage in open discussions about money management, including what risks they are willing to take. For example, parents might share their own experiences with investments, both successful and unsuccessful, providing valuable lessons for their children. Such conversations foster a culture of financial literacy that can be passed down through generations, ensuring that each family member is equipped to make informed decisions.

Moreover, learning from the successes and failures of others can provide invaluable insights. Take the tale of a seasoned investor who weathered multiple market downturns by adhering to a well-thought-out financial plan. His patience and resilience not only helped him recover but also allowed him to thrive when the market rebounded. This underscores the importance of perseverance and the ability to adapt one's strategy based on real-world experiences.

Ultimately, the journey of balancing risk and reward is not just about monetary gain; it is about building a legacy for future generations. Families who cultivate a mindset of strategic risk-taking can create wealth that lasts beyond their lifetime. By instilling these values in their children, they ensure that the lessons of financial wisdom are passed down, transforming the narrative from one of struggle to one of prosperity and stability. This generational wealth not only secures a better future but also empowers families to contribute positively to their communities, creating a ripple effect of financial education and success.

The Importance of Diversification

Diversification is a cornerstone of financial health, a principle that has been championed by investors for generations. Imagine a family that puts all their savings into a single venture, only to see it fail and their dreams vanish. This scenario is all too common, yet it can be avoided through the simple, yet powerful act of diversification. By spreading investments across various assets, individuals can mitigate risks and enhance their chances of long-term wealth accumulation. This fundamental strategy is not just reserved for the wealthy; it is accessible to everyone, regardless of their financial situation.

Consider the story of a young couple, Maria and John, who decided to take control of their financial future. They started with a modest savings account and slowly began to diversify their investments. By allocating funds to stocks, bonds, and mutual funds, they not only protected themselves against market volatility but also benefited from various growth potentials. Their journey illustrates that diversification is not merely a concept; it is a practical step that anyone can take to build a secure financial foundation for their family.

Science backs the benefits of diversification as well. Research has shown that a diversified portfolio can lead to improved risk-adjusted returns. The classic example is the correlation between different asset classes; when one asset is underperforming, another may thrive. This balancing act is crucial in maintaining financial stability over time. The concept can be likened to a well-orchestrated symphony, where different instruments come together to create a harmonious outcome, ensuring that no single note dominates the performance.

For those just starting on their financial journey, there are practical steps to achieve diversification. Begin by assessing your current financial situation and risk tolerance. From there, explore different types of investments, such as real estate, stocks, and even alternative assets like art or collectibles. Setting up automatic contributions to various investment accounts can also help in building a diversified portfolio without overwhelming yourself. Remember, the goal is to create a financial safety net that will support your family for generations to come.

In conclusion, the importance of diversification cannot be overstated. It is a strategy that empowers individuals and families to safeguard their financial future while fostering growth. By learning from the stories of those who have successfully diversified their investments and understanding the scientific principles behind it, anyone can take actionable steps toward financial freedom. Embracing this strategy not only benefits us today but also paves the way for our children and their children, ensuring that the wealth we build can last for generations.

Chapter 6: Generational Wealth Building

What is Generational Wealth?

Generational wealth is often described as the financial legacy that families build over time, allowing future generations to enjoy a higher standard of living without the struggle of starting from scratch. This concept is deeply rooted in the experiences of families who have successfully passed down assets, knowledge, and values that contribute to financial stability. For instance, consider a family that has owned a small business for decades. Through hard work and prudent financial management, they have not only built a profitable enterprise but have also instilled in their children the importance of financial literacy and entrepreneurship. This legacy enables the next generation to thrive, often leading to even greater successes.

At its core, generational wealth encompasses more than just money; it includes education, investments, and a mindset geared towards growth. Scientific studies have shown that families who prioritise financial education are more likely to create sustainable wealth. For example, a survey by the National Endowment for Financial Education revealed that children who are taught about money management are more likely to make sound financial decisions as adults. This highlights the importance of instilling financial wisdom early on, as it becomes a crucial component of wealth-building efforts.

Steps to creating generational wealth can begin with simple financial habits, such as budgeting, saving, and investing.

Families can start by setting financial goals together and discussing the importance of saving for both short-term needs and long-term investments. For instance, a family might decide to set aside a portion of their income each month specifically for educational savings accounts or retirement funds. This collective effort not only strengthens family bonds but also lays the groundwork for a financially secure future.

Moreover, storytelling plays a vital role in the transmission of generational wealth. Sharing personal narratives about financial successes and failures can serve as powerful lessons for younger generations. Take, for example, a grandparent who recounts their journey from poverty to prosperity, detailing the mistakes they made along the way. These stories not only inspire but also provide practical insights, making the concept of wealth more relatable and achievable for younger family members.

In conclusion, generational wealth is a multifaceted concept that includes financial assets, education, and shared values. By fostering an environment where financial literacy is prioritised and by encouraging open discussions about money, families can create a legacy that empowers future generations. The journey towards financial freedom may begin with small steps, but with dedication and commitment, it can lead to a wealth of opportunities that will benefit not only individuals but entire families for years to come.

Strategies for Passing Wealth to Future Generations

Passing wealth to future generations is not just about money; it's about instilling values, lessons, and a vision for financial responsibility. Many families have experienced the cycle of wealth accumulation and loss, often due to a lack of guidance. For example, consider the story of a successful entrepreneur who, after building a thriving business, realised that his children had little understanding of the value of money. He decided to change this by involving them in financial discussions, teaching them about investments, savings, and the importance of giving back. This approach not only secured their financial future but also reinforced family bonds and shared values.

One effective strategy for passing wealth is establishing a family trust. Trusts can protect assets and ensure they are distributed according to your wishes. A compelling case is that of a family who set up a trust to fund educational opportunities for their descendants. This not only secured their financial legacy but also encouraged a culture of learning and ambition within the family. By involving family members in the management of the trust, they learned valuable financial skills and the significance of responsible wealth management.

Education plays a crucial role in wealth transfer. Families should prioritise financial literacy by teaching children about budgeting, investing, and the principles of earning. A notable example includes a couple who created a financial education programme for their children, which included practical lessons on managing an allowance and setting savings goals. This proactive approach not only prepared their children for future financial challenges but also fostered a sense of accountability and independence.

Another essential strategy is open communication about finances. Many families avoid discussions about money, leading to misunderstandings and discord. A poignant story highlights a family that regularly held meetings to discuss financial matters, including their wealth management strategies. This transparency not only demystified finances for younger generations but also empowered them to engage with their family's financial legacy actively. By fostering a culture of openness, families can prevent conflicts and ensure a smoother transition of wealth.

Lastly, giving back to the community can strengthen family ties and instil a sense of purpose. Families who engage in charitable activities together often find that their collective experiences deepen their connections and enhance their understanding of wealth's role in society. For instance, one family established a foundation that allowed them to support local initiatives while involving their children in the decision-making process. This not only promoted philanthropy but also taught the younger generation that wealth should be used as a tool for positive change, ensuring that their legacy is not just about accumulation but also about contribution.

The Role of Education in Wealth Transfer

Education serves as a crucial pillar in the process of wealth transfer, shaping the mindset and financial literacy of future generations. For many families, knowledge about money management and investment strategies is not simply passed down; it is cultivated through education. Consider the story of a family that faced financial struggles, yet prioritised education. Their commitment led to their children excelling academically and eventually securing high-paying jobs, which in turn created a ripple effect, lifting the entire family out of poverty. This exemplifies how education can facilitate a transition from rags to riches.

Moreover, scientific studies have shown that individuals with higher education levels tend to accumulate more wealth over their lifetimes. This is not just due to the higher earning potential but also because educated individuals are more likely to engage in sound financial practices. They are equipped with critical thinking skills and the ability to navigate complex financial landscapes. For instance, a survey revealed that college graduates are significantly more likely to invest in stocks and retirement accounts than those without degrees, thereby enhancing their wealth-building capabilities.

The steps to harnessing the power of education for wealth transfer begin with instilling a love for learning in children from a young age. Parents can encourage curiosity and provide resources that promote financial literacy, such as books, workshops, and online courses. Involving children in family discussions about money can help demystify finances, making them more approachable. A family that educates its members about budgeting, saving, and investing can create a solid foundation for future wealth, ensuring that the cycle of financial struggle is broken.

Furthermore, community initiatives play a significant role in bridging the education gap. Many organisations offer financial education programmes tailored for families, fostering a culture of learning and empowerment. By participating in such initiatives, families can gain valuable insights and tools that are vital for wealth creation. A poignant example is a local community centre that transformed the lives of many families by providing free financial education workshops, resulting in increased savings and investment among participants.

Ultimately, the role of education in wealth transfer transcends mere academic achievement; it embodies a comprehensive approach to nurturing financial acumen across generations. It is about creating a legacy of knowledge that empowers individuals to make informed financial decisions. As families embrace education as a lifelong journey, they not only transform their financial futures but also contribute to a broader narrative of wealth and opportunity for all.

Chapter 7: Entrepreneurship as a Path to Wealth

Identifying Business Opportunities

Identifying business opportunities is the cornerstone of building generational wealth. Every successful entrepreneur starts with the ability to see gaps in the market. For instance, consider the story of a young woman in a small town who noticed a lack of healthy food options. She began by offering meal prep services using local ingredients. This simple idea grew into a thriving business, demonstrating that awareness of community needs can lead to significant financial success.

Science backs the notion that identifying opportunities often involves a mix of observation, research, and intuition. Studies have shown that those who engage in regular pattern recognition exercises, such as keeping a journal of their daily observations, often develop sharper business acumen. By training the mind to notice trends and changes in consumer behaviour, aspiring entrepreneurs can cultivate the skills necessary to spot lucrative opportunities where others might see obstacles.

Steps to identifying business opportunities include conducting market research, networking with industry professionals, and staying updated with global trends. For example, attending local business meet-ups can spark ideas and collaborations. One entrepreneur shared how a chance conversation at a networking event led to the launch of a product that filled a significant niche in eco-friendly packaging. These interactions can serve as a goldmine for inspiration and insight.

Moreover, it's crucial to embrace failure as part of the journey. The road to success is often paved with missteps, and learning from these experiences is vital. A father once told his children about his failed ventures before he finally succeeded. His story instilled resilience in them, teaching that every setback is merely a stepping stone towards identifying the right opportunity. This mindset not only nurtures perseverance but also encourages innovative thinking.

In conclusion, identifying business opportunities is not just about having a good idea; it involves a systematic approach to understanding market needs, leveraging personal experiences, and fostering connections. By following these steps and embracing both success and failure, anyone can pave their way towards financial freedom. Remember, each opportunity is a chance to build a legacy that can benefit generations to come.

Creating a Business Plan

Creating a business plan is a crucial step for anyone looking to achieve financial freedom and build generational wealth. It serves as a roadmap that guides entrepreneurs through the journey of turning their dreams into reality. For example, consider the story of a single mother who turned her baking hobby into a thriving cupcake business. By outlining her goals, target market, and financial projections, she successfully transformed her passion into a sustainable income, demonstrating that a well-thought-out plan can lead to remarkable outcomes.

The science behind effective business planning lies in understanding market dynamics and consumer behaviour.

Research shows that businesses with a clear plan are more likely to succeed than those that operate without one. This is because a solid business plan forces you to think critically about your market, competition, and unique value proposition. When you take the time to analyse these elements, you position yourself to make informed decisions that can propel your business forward. For instance, a family-owned farm that diversified its products based on market research saw a significant increase in profits and sustainability.

To create a business plan, start by defining your vision and mission. What do you want to achieve, and what values will guide your journey? Next, identify your target audience; knowing who will benefit from your product or service is essential in tailoring your offerings. Following this, conduct a SWOT analysis (Strengths, Weaknesses, Opportunities, Threats) to understand your position in the market. This structured approach not only clarifies your objectives but also identifies potential challenges that may arise.

Additionally, include financial projections in your business plan. This section should outline your expected income, expenses, and funding needs. Realistic financial forecasting helps you understand what resources are required and prepares you for future investments. For instance, a father who launched a tech startup by meticulously planning his budget and funding sources was able to secure investors and grow his business significantly within a few years, illustrating the importance of financial insight in planning.

Finally, remember that a business plan is not static; it should evolve as your business grows. Regularly revisiting and updating your plan ensures that you stay aligned with your goals and can adapt to changing market conditions. Embrace the journey of entrepreneurship with a flexible mindset and a commitment to learning. By doing so, you not only create a pathway to financial success for yourself but also set a powerful example for future generations, reinforcing the notion that financial freedom is achievable with the right planning and perseverance.

Overcoming Challenges in Entrepreneurship

Entrepreneurship is often seen as a path paved with excitement and potential riches, but the reality is far more complex. Many aspiring entrepreneurs face daunting challenges that can make the journey seem insurmountable. For instance, consider the story of Sarah, a single mother who started a small catering business. Initially, she struggled to balance her responsibilities with the demands of running a business, often working late into the night while managing her children's schedules. Her story illustrates the emotional and practical hurdles that many face when pursuing their dreams.

Moreover, the financial aspect of entrepreneurship can be overwhelming. Many entrepreneurs, like Sarah, find themselves constrained by limited resources, struggling to secure funding or manage expenses effectively. Research shows that nearly 30% of small businesses fail within the first two years due to cash flow issues. To overcome these challenges, it is crucial to develop a robust financial plan that includes budgeting and forecasting. This proactive approach can help in anticipating difficulties and preparing accordingly.

Networking also plays a vital role in overcoming entrepreneurial challenges. Building connections with mentors and like-minded individuals can provide invaluable support and advice. For example, Sarah joined a local business association, where she met seasoned entrepreneurs who shared their experiences and offered guidance. This sense of community not only provided practical help but also emotional encouragement, reminding her that she was not alone in her struggles.

In addition to seeking support, resilience is key to overcoming setbacks in entrepreneurship. Each failure can be viewed as a learning opportunity. Studies have shown that resilience can be developed through practice and a positive mindset. For Sarah, every setback—whether it was a poorly attended event or a dissatisfied customer—became a lesson that strengthened her resolve and improved her business acumen.

Finally, setting realistic goals is essential for maintaining motivation and focus. Entrepreneurs should break down their larger objectives into smaller, manageable steps. This method can prevent feelings of overwhelm and provide a clearer path to success. For Sarah, setting a goal to increase her customer base by 10% each month allowed her to celebrate small victories along the way, ultimately leading to the long-term success she envisioned. By understanding and addressing these challenges, aspiring entrepreneurs can navigate their journey more effectively, paving the way for financial freedom and generational wealth.

Chapter 8: The Role of Real Estate

Understanding Real Estate Investment

Real estate investment stands as a beacon of hope for families aspiring to secure their financial future. Imagine a young couple, Sarah and James, who started with nothing but a modest apartment. With determination and some research, they purchased their first rental property. Over the years, this investment not only provided them with additional income but also grew in value, allowing them to upgrade their lifestyle and save for their children's education. Their story illustrates how real estate can be a powerful tool for building wealth.

Understanding the basics of real estate investment is crucial for anyone considering this path. At its core, real estate investment involves purchasing property with the expectation that it will generate income or appreciate in value. But it is not just about the numbers; it's about creating a legacy. Research shows that real estate has historically outperformed other asset classes over the long term. Families can leverage this asset to create multi-generational wealth, ensuring that future generations benefit from their predecessors' hard work.

The journey of investing in real estate can be broken down into manageable steps. First, one must educate themselves about the market dynamics, financing options, and property management. For instance, attending local property seminars or engaging with experienced investors can provide invaluable insights. Next, aspiring investors should set clear financial goals and determine their risk tolerance. This clarity will guide their decisions as they navigate potential properties. Ultimately, taking informed steps can mitigate risks and enhance the likelihood of success.

Moreover, the emotional aspect of real estate investment cannot be overlooked. Families often invest not just for financial gain but for the security and stability that owning property can provide. Consider the story of the Martins, who purchased a home in a good neighbourhood, fostering a sense of community for their children. This emotional connection can be a motivating factor, driving families to make wise investment choices that align with their values and aspirations.

In conclusion, understanding real estate investment is more than just a financial decision; it's a step towards creating a legacy of wealth that can last for generations. By following the stories of those who have succeeded, educating themselves, and making strategic choices, families can unlock the potential of real estate. The path may be challenging, but the rewards of financial freedom and security are well worth the effort. As we delve deeper into this guide, let us explore more strategies to ensure that every family can embark on this transformative journey.

The Benefits of Property Ownership

Owning property is one of the most powerful means to build generational wealth. It serves not only as a place to live but also as an investment that appreciates over time. For instance, consider the story of a family that purchased their first home in a modest neighbourhood. With each passing year, the value of the property rose, allowing them to sell it for a substantial profit. This profit then became the seed money for their next investment, illustrating how property ownership can set the foundation for future financial stability.

Moreover, property ownership provides a sense of security and belonging. When you own your home, you have control over your environment and can create a space that reflects your family's values and traditions. This emotional connection often leads to a stronger family unit, as generations grow up in a stable environment. For many, owning a home is a dream realised, representing years of hard work and sacrifice, which further solidifies the importance of property as a cornerstone of wealth.

Financially, real estate can be a hedge against inflation. As prices rise, so too does the value of owned properties, making them a smart investment choice. A family that invested in a rental property a decade ago likely saw not just appreciation in value but also a steady stream of income from tenants. This dual benefit showcases how property ownership can diversify income streams and enhance financial resilience, providing families with greater peace of mind during uncertain economic times.

Additionally, property ownership often comes with tax advantages that can significantly enhance wealth-building efforts. Homeowners can deduct mortgage interest and property taxes, resulting in savings that can be reinvested. Consider a couple that used their tax savings to invest in further property or education for their children, thereby creating a cycle of wealth that can last for generations.

Understanding these financial benefits can empower families to make informed decisions about their investments.

Lastly, the act of owning property fosters a sense of responsibility and stewardship. Families often take pride in maintaining their homes and communities, which can lead to local improvements and increased property values. When families invest in their surroundings, they not only elevate their own financial situation but also contribute to the betterment of society as a whole. This collective effort can create a ripple effect, inspiring others to invest in their futures through property ownership, ultimately fostering a culture of wealth building.

Navigating the Real Estate Market

Navigating the real estate market requires a blend of intuition, research, and strategic planning. Many families have transformed their financial standing by understanding the dynamics of property investment. Take the story of the Johnsons, who, with limited resources, purchased their first home in a burgeoning neighbourhood. By conducting thorough research on market trends and property values, they not only secured a comfortable living space but also laid the groundwork for generational wealth that would benefit their children and grandchildren.

The science behind real estate investment is rooted in understanding cycles. Real estate markets ebb and flow, influenced by economic factors, interest rates, and local demand. Families should educate themselves on these cycles to make informed decisions. The Johnsons, for instance, recognised that purchasing during a market downturn provided them with significant equity, allowing them to invest further. This knowledge is crucial for anyone looking to build wealth through property.

Steps to navigate the real estate market effectively include setting clear financial goals, researching local markets, and understanding financing options. Families should start with a budget that includes not only the purchase price but also taxes, maintenance, and potential renovations. The Johnsons created a detailed financial plan, enabling them to make a competitive offer on their home without overextending themselves, illustrating the importance of discipline in property investment.

Networking within the community can also open doors to hidden opportunities. Engaging with local real estate agents, attending community events, or joining property investment groups can provide valuable insights. The Johnsons found their ideal home through a community connection, demonstrating how relationships can lead to advantageous deals. This highlights that successful navigation of the real estate market is not solely about numbers; it's also about people.

Ultimately, navigating the real estate market is a journey that can lead to financial freedom and generational wealth. It requires commitment, education, and a willingness to adapt. Families like the Johnsons exemplify the potential of property investment when approached with diligence and care. By leveraging knowledge and fostering relationships, anyone can embark on their path to financial success through real estate, creating a legacy that endures for generations.

Chapter 9: Financial Tools and Resources

Banking and Credit Options

In the journey from rags to riches, understanding banking and credit options can be pivotal to achieving financial stability and prosperity. Many families, regardless of their starting point, can benefit from being well-informed about the various banking services available. These services, including savings accounts, loans, and investment options, are the building blocks of financial freedom. Take the story of the Smith family, who, after years of struggling, discovered the potential of a simple savings account, which not only helped them manage their day-to-day expenses but also allowed them to accumulate funds for their children's education.

Credit plays a significant role in shaping one's financial landscape. It can be a double-edged sword; if used wisely, it can open doors to opportunities such as home ownership and business ventures. However, poor credit management can lead to a cycle of debt that is challenging to escape. Consider the experience of Maria, who after a few missteps, learned the importance of her credit score. By diligently paying off debts and utilising credit responsibly, she transformed her financial standing, proving that understanding credit is crucial for long-term wealth accumulation.

The science of banking and credit is rooted in understanding interest rates and terms. Families must educate themselves about the fine print of loans and credit agreements.

For instance, the Johnsons took the time to read through their mortgage agreement, which unveiled hidden fees that could have cost them thousands in the long run. By being proactive and asking questions, they were empowered to negotiate better terms on their loan, highlighting the importance of being informed and vigilant in financial dealings.

Steps to navigate banking and credit options include setting clear financial goals, researching various institutions, and seeking advice when necessary. Families should consider visiting local community banks or credit unions, which often provide personalised services and lower fees compared to larger banks. The Garcia family found success by consulting with a financial advisor, who helped them craft a tailored financial plan that included a mix of savings, investments, and responsible borrowing. This approach not only provided them with immediate benefits but also laid a strong foundation for generational wealth.

Ultimately, the path to financial freedom through banking and credit is accessible to everyone willing to learn and take action. The stories of families like the Smiths, Marias, and Johnsons serve as powerful reminders that with the right knowledge and tools, anyone can transform their financial situation. By embracing the principles of smart banking and responsible credit management, families can not only improve their current circumstances but also create a legacy of wealth for future generations.

Financial Advisors: When and How to Use Them

In today's complex financial landscape, the role of financial advisors has become increasingly essential for individuals seeking to build and preserve wealth. Many people are unsure about when to engage a financial advisor, often waiting until a crisis arises or when they have accumulated a significant amount of assets. However, the truth is that the best time to consult an advisor is before you reach that tipping point. By seeking their guidance early, you can establish a solid financial foundation and prevent potential pitfalls along the way.

Consider the story of the Johnson family, who sought the help of a financial advisor when they were expecting their first child. They wanted to ensure they were making the right decisions regarding their savings and investments. With the advisor's assistance, they created a comprehensive financial plan that included saving for their child's education and planning for retirement simultaneously. This proactive approach allowed them to feel confident about their financial future, demonstrating the power of early intervention.

Financial advisors offer more than just investment advice; they also provide insights into budgeting, tax strategies, and estate planning. Research shows that individuals who work with financial professionals tend to achieve better financial outcomes than those who navigate their finances alone. This is particularly important for families looking to create generational wealth, as sound financial planning can lead to lasting prosperity for future generations. By leveraging the expertise of a financial advisor, families can ensure that their wealth is not only accumulated but effectively passed down.

When considering how to utilise a financial advisor, it's vital to understand the various types available. Some specialise in retirement planning, while others focus on wealth management or tax strategies. Selecting the right advisor depends on your specific needs and financial goals. It's advisable to conduct thorough research, seek recommendations, and interview potential advisors to find someone who aligns with your values and objectives. This step is crucial in establishing a productive and trusting relationship.

Ultimately, the journey towards financial freedom is a marathon, not a sprint. Engaging a financial advisor can be a significant step in ensuring that you are on the right track. Whether you're just starting out or looking to refine your existing strategy, the insights and support of a professional can help you navigate the often tumultuous waters of personal finance. Remember, the earlier you seek guidance, the more opportunities you have to set the stage for lasting wealth and success for your family.

Technology in Finance: Apps and Software

In the modern world, technology has transformed the way we handle finances, making it more accessible and manageable for everyone. Apps and software tailored for financial management have become essential tools for families seeking to achieve financial freedom. For instance, a young couple might use budgeting apps to track their spending and savings goals, ensuring they stay on course towards their dream of home ownership. These digital tools not only simplify finance management but also empower users to make informed decisions about their money.

Moreover, the rise of investment apps has opened doors for a new generation of investors. With just a few taps on a smartphone, anyone can start investing in stocks or mutual funds, regardless of their financial background. Stories abound of individuals who, once hesitant to dive into the stock market, now confidently build their portfolios using these user-friendly platforms. This accessibility fosters a more inclusive financial landscape where everyone has the opportunity to grow their wealth.

Additionally, financial software designed for long-term planning has become indispensable in building generational wealth. Families are now equipped with tools that help them project future expenses, plan for education, and even strategise for retirement. A family could use these tools to simulate various financial scenarios, ultimately leading to better preparation for life's uncertainties. By leveraging technology, they can create a roadmap that not only secures their financial future but also lays the groundwork for the prosperity of their children and grandchildren.

Furthermore, the integration of artificial intelligence in finance apps has enhanced the user experience, providing tailored advice based on individual financial habits. Imagine a scenario where a parent receives real-time suggestions on how to save for their child's education or tips on reducing unnecessary expenses. Such personalised guidance makes financial management less daunting and more achievable. It’s not just about having the tools but also about having them work for you, propelling you towards your financial goals.

In conclusion, the impact of technology on finance is profound and transformative. As families embrace these apps and software, they are not just managing their current finances but are actively participating in a journey towards financial independence. The stories of those who have successfully navigated this landscape serve as motivation for others to do the same. With the right tools in hand, anyone can start their journey towards building generational wealth, ensuring that the next generation has a stronger financial foundation to build upon.

Chapter 10: Maintaining Wealth

The Importance of Continual Learning

In today's fast-paced world, the importance of continual learning cannot be overstated. Each day brings new challenges and opportunities, and those who commit to learning are better equipped to navigate these changes. Take the story of a young entrepreneur who, despite facing numerous setbacks, dedicated herself to learning new skills. She attended workshops, read extensively, and sought mentorship. Over time, her perseverance paid off, turning her small startup into a thriving enterprise. Her journey exemplifies how continual learning can lead to financial success and personal growth.

Science supports the notion that continual learning not only enhances skills but also boosts cognitive function. Research shows that engaging in lifelong learning can increase brain plasticity, making it easier to adapt to new situations and solve complex problems. When individuals actively seek knowledge, they are more likely to innovate and find creative solutions to financial challenges. This scientific understanding reinforces the idea that learning is not just an activity but a crucial investment in one's future.

To foster a culture of continual learning, families can implement specific steps. Setting aside time each week for educational activities, such as reading books or attending online courses, can cultivate a learning environment. Families can also engage in discussions about financial literacy, encouraging all members to share their insights and questions.

By prioritising education, families not only enhance their financial acumen but also strengthen their bonds through shared experiences.

Moreover, continual learning is key to building generational wealth. Parents who model a commitment to education instil the same values in their children, creating a legacy of knowledge and financial wisdom. For instance, a family that regularly discusses investments and savings strategies equips its younger members with the tools they need to succeed. This proactive approach ensures that financial knowledge is passed down, allowing future generations to thrive.

In conclusion, the journey from rags to riches is paved with the bricks of continual learning. Those who embrace this journey are more likely to overcome obstacles and achieve financial freedom. As we advance into an increasingly complex world, the ability to learn and adapt will be the cornerstone of success. By recognising the value of education and making it a priority, families can secure not just their financial future but a legacy that inspires generations to come.

Protecting Your Wealth: Insurance and Legal Tools

In today's uncertain world, protecting your wealth is paramount. Insurance and legal tools serve as shields against unforeseen events that could jeopardise your hard-earned assets. Imagine a family who, after years of diligent saving and investing, faced a devastating fire that destroyed their home. Without adequate insurance, they would have been left with nothing, but with the right coverage, they could rebuild and secure their future. This story exemplifies the importance of having a robust safety net that allows for recovery and continuity in the face of adversity.

Legal tools, such as wills and trusts, are equally crucial in safeguarding generational wealth. A well-structured will ensures that your assets are distributed according to your wishes, preventing family disputes and financial chaos after you're gone. Consider the tale of a wealthy entrepreneur who neglected to draft a will. Upon his passing, his family faced bitter legal battles, ultimately leading to the depletion of his estate. By planning ahead and utilising legal instruments, families can preserve their legacy and ensure that future generations benefit from the wealth painstakingly built over time.

Insurance is not just about protecting physical assets; it also encompasses health and life coverage. A sudden illness or accident can drain finances, leaving families in dire straits. A relatable story is of a young couple who invested in comprehensive health insurance. When one partner fell seriously ill, their insurance covered medical expenses, allowing them to focus on healing rather than worrying about bills. This highlights that having the right insurance can provide peace of mind and financial stability when it matters most.

Moreover, understanding the various types of insurance available is essential. From property and casualty to life and health insurance, each type serves a unique purpose. Families should assess their needs and consider factors such as lifestyle, financial goals, and risk tolerance. A systematic approach to selecting the right insurance can lead to significant savings and enhanced protection, ensuring that families are well-prepared for any eventuality.

In conclusion, protecting your wealth with insurance and legal tools is not just a necessity; it is a critical step towards financial freedom. By learning from stories of others and applying practical steps, families can create a solid foundation for their wealth. The journey from rags to riches is not solely about accumulating assets; it is equally about safeguarding what you have for future generations. With the right planning and protection in place, you can ensure that your family thrives long after you are gone.

Giving Back: Philanthropy and Community Impact

Philanthropy is more than just a charitable act; it is a powerful tool that can transform communities and empower generations. When families who have achieved financial success choose to give back, they create ripples of change that extend far beyond their own wealth. For instance, consider the story of an entrepreneur who, after selling his business, established a foundation to support local education initiatives. This act not only provided resources for schools in underserved areas but also inspired others in his community to invest in the future of children, demonstrating how one person's commitment can ignite a collective effort.

The science behind philanthropy reveals its profound impact on both the giver and the receiver. Research shows that individuals who engage in charitable giving experience a boost in happiness and well-being. The act of giving fosters a sense of purpose and connection, reminding us of our shared humanity. Moreover, when families involve their children in philanthropic activities, they instil values of empathy, responsibility, and community service. This lays the groundwork for a legacy of generosity, teaching future generations that wealth is not solely for personal gain but also for uplifting others.

Taking actionable steps towards philanthropy involves identifying causes that resonate personally with one's values. Families can start small by volunteering time or resources to local charities, or they can engage in larger initiatives such as setting up scholarship funds or community projects. Creating a family mission statement around giving can unite members in a common goal, making philanthropy a shared journey. As families grow together in their giving efforts, they not only strengthen their bonds but also build a culture of giving that can last for generations.

The impact of philanthropy extends beyond financial donations; it also includes time, knowledge, and skills. Families can leverage their unique talents to mentor others, providing guidance and support to those embarking on their own paths to success. For example, a family with expertise in business can host workshops to teach entrepreneurship to young adults in their community. This kind of engagement empowers individuals to break free from the cycle of poverty, fostering a sense of agency and hope.

Ultimately, giving back is a vital component of the journey from rags to riches. By understanding the importance of philanthropy, families can harness their wealth to create lasting change. The stories of impactful giving not only inspire but also serve as blueprints for those who wish to emulate similar successes. As families embrace the role of benefactors, they not only elevate their own lives but also contribute to the flourishing of their communities, ensuring that the legacy of generosity continues to thrive for generations to come.

Chapter 11: Real-Life Stories of Success

Inspiring Tales of Financial Transformation

In the heart of every financial success story lies a tale of transformation. Take the journey of Sarah, a single mother who turned her life around after facing eviction. With limited resources, she discovered budgeting tools online and began to track her spending meticulously. Over time, she learned to prioritise her needs over wants, and her disciplined approach allowed her to save enough for a deposit on a modest home, providing stability for her children and a foundation for future wealth.

Similarly, consider the inspiring tale of James, who grew up in a low-income neighbourhood but had big dreams. He realised early on that education was his ticket to a better life. By working part-time jobs and applying for scholarships, he earned a degree in finance. Today, he shares his financial knowledge with others in his community, empowering them to seek opportunities, invest wisely, and build generational wealth.

Research supports these narratives, showing that financial literacy is key to breaking the cycle of poverty. Studies indicate that families who engage in financial education are more likely to create budgets, save, and invest. By understanding the science of money management, individuals can transform their financial realities, paving the way for future generations to thrive. These stories exemplify how knowledge can be a powerful tool in achieving financial freedom.

Steps to financial transformation often begin with small, manageable changes. Establishing a budget, setting savings goals, and tracking progress can lead to significant results over time. Additionally, seeking mentorship or community support can provide the encouragement needed to stay motivated. These incremental steps create a ripple effect, inspiring others to take charge of their financial destinies and cultivate wealth for their families.

Ultimately, the tales of Sarah and James remind us that financial transformation is possible for anyone willing to take the first step. By sharing their stories and the science behind their success, we can foster a global movement towards financial literacy and empowerment. Each of us holds the potential to rewrite our financial stories, ensuring that future generations inherit not just wealth, but the wisdom to manage it effectively.

Lessons Learned from Failure

Failure is often seen as a setback, but it can actually be a powerful teacher. Every successful individual has faced challenges that initially seemed insurmountable. Take the story of J.K. Rowling, for example, who faced numerous rejections before the Harry Potter series became a global phenomenon. Her experience illustrates that the road to success is often littered with failures that ultimately shape our resilience and determination. Learning from these experiences can help us to forge a path toward financial freedom for ourselves and our families.

In the realm of personal finance, it is essential to understand that mistakes are part of the journey. Many individuals fall into the trap of believing that financial literacy comes naturally, but the reality is that it is learned through trial and error. Research shows that people who reflect on their financial missteps tend to make better decisions in the future. By analysing what went wrong, whether it was overspending or poor investment choices, we can develop a more robust financial strategy that not only benefits us but also sets a precedent for future generations.

A key lesson from failure is the importance of adaptability. When faced with financial difficulties, the ability to pivot and change course can make all the difference. For instance, consider the story of a family that lost their home due to unforeseen circumstances. Instead of succumbing to despair, they reassessed their financial priorities, sought education on budgeting, and ultimately rebuilt their lives. This adaptability not only helped them recover but also instilled a sense of financial responsibility that they passed on to their children.

Moreover, sharing our failures with others can foster a supportive community. By discussing our financial blunders openly, we can help others avoid similar pitfalls. This communal approach creates an environment where individuals feel empowered to ask questions and seek advice, which is crucial for building generational wealth. The importance of mentorship cannot be overstated; learning from the experiences of those who have walked the path before us can illuminate our journey toward financial success.

Finally, embracing a growth mindset is pivotal in transforming failure into success. This perspective allows us to view setbacks not as the end of the road but as a crucial stepping stone towards achieving our financial goals. By celebrating small victories and acknowledging the lessons learned from failures, we can cultivate a positive financial outlook that inspires ourselves and our families. The journey to financial freedom is not a straight line, but with perseverance and the right mindset, we can navigate it successfully together.

The Impact of Community and Support

In the journey from rags to riches, the role of community and support cannot be overstated. Families that cultivate strong networks often find themselves better equipped to handle financial challenges. For instance, consider a single mother who, despite her struggles, connects with a local support group. This group not only provides emotional backing but also shares financial resources, tips, and strategies that help her pave the way towards financial independence. Such communal ties can transform daunting obstacles into manageable tasks.

Research indicates that individuals with robust social networks are more likely to achieve their financial goals. A study by the American Psychological Association revealed that people who engage with supportive communities report higher levels of motivation and resilience. This is particularly crucial in times of economic downturn, where the collective strength of a community can inspire innovative solutions and collaborative efforts. When families unite, they create a ripple effect, encouraging one another to aspire for greater financial stability.

The emotional aspect of community support also plays a critical role. When individuals feel they are part of a group that genuinely cares, their mental wellbeing improves, which in turn affects their financial decisions. For example, a family that shares their financial struggles openly within a community is more likely to receive constructive advice and encouragement. This safe space fosters vulnerability and honesty, allowing families to work through their issues together, leading to better financial outcomes.

To cultivate such a supportive environment, families can take proactive steps. Joining local groups, participating in workshops, or even creating online forums dedicated to financial literacy can make a significant difference. Additionally, fostering inter-generational connections—where older family members share their financial wisdom with younger ones—can create a legacy of learning and growth. These actions not only strengthen family bonds but also equip future generations with the tools needed to build and sustain wealth.

Ultimately, the impact of community and support on financial prosperity is profound. It is not merely about pooling resources; it is about nurturing relationships that empower individuals and families to thrive. By investing time and effort into building a supportive network, families can overcome financial hurdles together, transforming their dreams of wealth into reality. The journey may be challenging, but with the right community, the path to financial freedom becomes not just a possibility but a shared adventure.

Chapter 12: Creating Your Family Wealth Plan

Assessing Your Current Financial Situation

Assessing your current financial situation is a crucial first step on the journey to financial freedom. Many families overlook this fundamental process, often feeling overwhelmed by numbers or intimidated by their financial past. Picture a family sitting around the dining table, each member sharing their financial concerns and dreams. This open dialogue can reveal the hidden fears and aspirations that shape their financial reality. By encouraging honest communication, families can better understand their starting point and create a unified plan for improvement.

Once the conversation begins, it's essential to gather clear data on income, expenses, debts, and assets. This process is akin to taking an inventory before embarking on a long journey. Just as a traveller wouldn't set off without checking their map and supplies, a family should not pursue financial goals without a thorough understanding of their current situation. Tools like budgeting apps or simple spreadsheets can make this task less daunting. The key is to be meticulous and honest about every penny, as this transparency lays the foundation for future financial decisions.

After collecting the necessary data, it's important to analyse it thoughtfully. Families may discover surprising patterns in their spending habits, akin to a detective piecing together clues in a mystery. For example, a family might find that they are spending excessively on dining out, which could be redirected towards savings or investment. This revelation can lead to empowering changes, as families can make informed decisions that align with their overall financial goals. The process of analysing one's financial situation not only highlights areas for improvement but also fosters a sense of control and responsibility.

In addition to assessing the numbers, it's vital to consider the emotional aspects of finances. Money often carries a significant emotional weight, tied to personal experiences and family values. For instance, a story of a grandmother who saved diligently during hard times can inspire younger generations to appreciate the importance of financial discipline. Recognising these emotional ties can motivate families to create meaningful financial goals that resonate on a deeper level. Understanding the psychology behind spending and saving can transform the way families approach their finances.

Finally, creating an action plan based on the assessment is essential for moving forward. This plan should encompass specific, measurable, achievable, relevant, and time-bound (SMART) goals. Families can work together to set milestones, whether it's paying off a debt, saving for a holiday, or investing for the future. Celebrating small victories along the way can foster a sense of unity and accomplishment. As families embark on this journey from rags to riches, they will find that every step taken in assessing and improving their financial situation brings them closer to lasting generational wealth.

Engaging Your Family in Financial Discussions

Engaging your family in financial discussions is a vital step towards building a legacy of wealth and understanding. Many families shy away from these conversations, often due to discomfort or a lack of knowledge. However, sharing financial information can strengthen bonds and empower every member of the family. Consider the story of the Johnsons, who turned their financial struggles into family discussions that led to a newfound appreciation for budgeting and saving, ultimately paving the way for a brighter financial future.

Start by creating a safe space for dialogue. Choose a relaxed environment, like a family dinner or a weekend outing, where everyone feels comfortable sharing their thoughts. Introduce the topic gently, perhaps by discussing a recent news article about financial literacy. This can serve as an icebreaker and encourage family members to voice their opinions. Research shows that families who communicate openly about finances tend to make better financial decisions together, fostering a sense of unity and shared purpose.

Next, involve everyone in the planning process. Assign age-appropriate financial tasks to each family member, such as tracking expenses or researching investment options. This hands-on approach not only educates but also instils a sense of responsibility and ownership. For example, the Smith family implemented a monthly 'financial family night' where each member presented their findings on savings strategies or investment opportunities, leading to exciting discussions and collective decision-making.

Utilise storytelling to make financial concepts relatable and engaging. Share personal anecdotes or historical examples that highlight the importance of financial literacy. This could include tales of ancestors who built wealth through hard work and wise investments. Scientific studies indicate that storytelling can enhance understanding and retention of information, making it an effective tool in financial education.

Finally, celebrate financial milestones together, no matter how small. Acknowledge when the family reaches a savings goal or successfully implements a new budgeting system. This not only reinforces positive behaviour but also creates a culture of achievement within the family. The Garcias, for instance, celebrated their debt-free status with a family trip, solidifying their commitment to financial freedom and leaving a lasting impact on their children's attitudes towards money. By engaging your family in financial discussions, you lay the groundwork for generational wealth and a legacy of informed financial decision-making.

Building a Legacy of Wealth and Values

Building a legacy of wealth and values begins with a vision that transcends generations. It's not merely about accumulating money, but rather about instilling principles that guide future generations toward responsible financial stewardship. For instance, consider the story of a family that prioritised education and community service alongside financial success. By fostering a culture of giving back, they not only grew their wealth but also built a legacy that inspired others to follow suit.

Scientific research supports the notion that values play a crucial role in financial behaviours. Studies have shown that families who communicate openly about money and instill strong values in their children often see better financial outcomes. This is exemplified by families who engage in regular discussions about budgeting, saving, and the importance of making informed financial choices. By incorporating these discussions into family life, they create a shared understanding of wealth that aligns with their values.

Taking actionable steps to build this legacy is essential. Families can start by creating a family mission statement that outlines their financial goals and core values. This statement serves as a guiding light, helping to navigate financial decisions and ensuring that wealth is built and maintained in alignment with their beliefs. In addition, engaging in activities such as family investment meetings can strengthen bonds and enhance financial literacy among all members.

Moreover, passing on financial knowledge is as important as the wealth itself. For example, teaching children how to manage an allowance or encouraging them to take part in family investment projects can lay the groundwork for responsible money habits. These experiences not only empower the younger generation but also reinforce the values that underpin the family's wealth-building efforts.

Ultimately, building a legacy of wealth and values is about creating a holistic approach to financial freedom. By intertwining financial success with strong ethical principles, families can ensure that their legacy endures beyond monetary wealth. As seen in the stories of those who have successfully navigated this journey, it is the values imparted alongside the wealth that truly define their legacy, inspiring others to achieve their own financial freedom while remaining grounded in their core beliefs. It's a beautiful day.

- AUTHOR RICHARD TRILLION MANTEY

www.ingramcontent.com/pod-product-compliance
Lightning Source LLC
LaVergne TN
LVHW022314200926
848481LV00004B/1339